Asi
Veget
RECIPES

Your Promise of Success

Welcome to the world of Confident Cooking, created for you in our
test kitchen, where recipes are double-tested by our team of home
economists to achieve a high standard of success.

PERIPLUS

Glossary

Bean curd skin sheets: made from soy beans, this is the dried skin which forms on the surface of soy bean milk when it is allowed to stand. It is used as a wrapping to enclose savoury fillings.

Betel leaves: are the leaves of the betel pepper and are used in Indian, Thai and Malaysian cooking. Available fresh in Asian food stores, they are used to wrap around small pieces of food. They are often cooked quickly or soaked in water and sugar to slightly soften the leaf before use.

Brown mustard seeds: these are sold whole in supermarkets, and some Asian food stores. They are used in oriental cooking.

Chilli paste and jam: are both available in Asian food stores. They are made with tomato, onion, chilli, oil, tamarind, garlic, sugar, salt, spices and vinegar. For vegetarian cooking, check the label to ensure the brand you buy does not contain shrimp paste.

Bean sauce: a dark paste-like sauce made from soy beans, sesame oil, wheat flour, sugar and salt. It is used in Chinese cuisine as a base for flavouring dishes and should be used sparingly due to its high salty flavour. Bean sauce is available in Asian food stores and supermarkets.

Black sesame seeds: have an earthy taste when in their raw state. They are mainly used in desserts but can be toasted and used in savoury dishes. Cover the seeds slightly if toasting, as they tend to pop.

Besan flour: is made from ground chickpeas and is used in Indian cuisine as a coating for fritters and as a thickener. Besan flour has a distinctive flavour. It is available from health food shops and some larger supermarkets.

Bok choy (also Chinese chard or Chinese white cabbage): has fleshy white stems and dark-green curly leaves. It has a slight mustardy taste. There is also a smaller version called Shanghai or baby bok choy.

Chinese rice wine (or Shaosing): is amber-coloured with a rich, sweetish taste. Use dry sherry if not available, but grape wines are not suitable.

2

Coconut cream and milk: are both extracted from the grated flesh of mature coconuts—cream is rich and thick and rises to the surface, while the milk is underneath. When a recipe uses cream, don't shake the can, but use the thick cream on top.

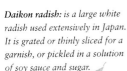

Daikon radish: is a large white radish used extensively in Japan. It is grated or thinly sliced for a garnish, or pickled in a solution of soy sauce and sugar.

Dried bamboo leaves: a dried greeny brown leaf about 40 cm in length. Available in packets from Asian food stores.

Dried rice vermicelli: are clear thread-like rice sticks. When cooked they develop a slippery texture and absorb flavours of other food. Soak in hot water and drain well before use.

Ghee: clarified unsalted butter reaches high temperatures before it smokes, unlike other oils and fats. Used in Indian cooking.

Glutinous rice: is available in white and black grains. It becomes sticky when cooked, is often used as a dessert rice and is soaked before cooking. The white variety is also served with savoury dishes.

Gow gee wrappers: are round pieces of dough made from wheat flour and water. These wrappers are usually used in steamed dishes.

Green papaya: is not a different variety, but an underripe fruit—if the papaya is too green it will be bitter. It is commonly used in Asian salads and some soups, or as a snack with sugar and chilli.

Japanese soy sauce (also called shoyu): this is much lighter and sweeter than Chinese soy sauce. It is naturally brewed, so refrigerate after opening.

Kaffir lime leaves: are from the kaffir lime—a knobbly, dark-skinned lime with a very strong fragrance and flavour. Fresh leaves are dark green, shiny double leaves, with a very pungent perfume. They are quite thick and must be sliced very finely when making curry pastes and salads, but are left whole in curries.

Konbu (also called sea vegetable or hidaka): is a dried broad dark-green seaweed leaf. It is rinsed and cooked in water to extract the sea flavour. The konbu is discarded after cooking and the liquid is then used as a base flavour in Japanese dishes.

Nori sheets: *a marine algae found on the surface of the sea off Japan, China and Korea. It is formed into paper-like sheets, compressed and then dried. Its colour ranges from green to purple. It is used in Japan to wrap around rice and various fillings to make sushi.*

Rice paper (or bahn tran in Vietnamese): *are thin sheets made from rice flour, water and salt with a basket-weave texture. They're purchased dry in sealed packets and will keep indefinitely in this state—handle carefully as they are brittle and may shatter if dropped. Moisten in hot water before use.*

Sambal oelek: *is a hot paste made from fresh red chillies, mashed and mixed with salt. It is used as a relish in Indonesian and Malaysian cooking and can be used as a substitute for fresh chillies in most recipes. It will keep, sealed, for months in the refrigerator.*

Pickled ginger: *is a distinctive feature of Japanese cuisine and has a very sharp taste. There are a variety of pickled gingers on the market, either in brine or sweet vinegars. It is used as an accompaniment to sushi and sashimi and acts as a palate cleanser.*

Rice vinegar and seasoned rice vinegar: *rice vinegar is made from vinegar and a natural rice extract—seasoned rice vinegar has sugar and salt added. Used in dressings and marinades.*

Shiitake mushrooms: *are a variety of fungus which are commonly used in Japanese and Chinese recipes. They are available in both dried and fresh form. Dried shiitake mushrooms must be soaked before use and their woody stems discarded. The soaking liquid can be used as a stock or flavouring.*

Rice flour: *is used as a thickening agent in some Asian dishes. Rice flour is ground from whole rice and rice pieces. It is available from most supermarkets. Once opened it can be stored indefinitely in an airtight container.*

Sake: *an alcoholic liquid made by fermenting cooked ground rice mash. It has a sherry-like taste and is used as a drink and a cooking liquid. Available clear and amber in colour.*

Soba noodles: *are made from buckwheat flour and are available both dried and fresh—fresh soba noodles have a chewy texture. They are used in hot noodle soups and in cold dishes.*

Spring roll wrappers: are square pieces of dough, available in different sizes, fresh or frozen. They are used to make many wrapped snacks such as spring rolls. They need longer to cook than won ton wrappers and are mainly used for deep-frying.

Tamari: a naturally fermented dark soy sauce with a flavour stronger than Japanese soy sauce (or shoyu). There are some varieties available that are wheat-free.

Tamarind: is a large brown bean-like pod with a fruity, tart flavour. It is available as a dried shelled fruit, as a block of compressed pulp (usually containing seeds), or as a purèe or concentrate. It is often added to Indian and Thai curries.

Tatsoi lettuce (also called brassica junea or rosette bok choy): is a variety of bok choy and has a delicate flavour. This small oriental vegetable has flat, rosette, dark-green leaves and is eaten raw or in stir-fries.

Tempeh: is made from the soya bean. The difference between tofu and tempeh is that tempeh is fermented (like miso and soy sauce). It is made by adding a culture to the cooked soya beans and then compressed into firm blocks. As tempeh is bland in itself, it is often available marinated in a mixture of spices.

Thai basil leaves: have a strong aroma and are used extensively in Asian cooking. The green and purple serrated edge leaves branch from a purple stem. The flowers are pink. The leaves are added to Thai curries and stir-fries at the end of cooking. Also used in Vietnamese cooking as a garnish for soups.

Tofu (firm): is still soft, but will hold its shape during cooking. It is suitable for stir-frying, pan-frying, marinating and baking.

Tofu (fried puffs): the tofu is treated differently to other tofu to give it an aerated texture and is then deep-fried. It is suitable for stir-fries, curries and soups.

Tofu (hard): is slightly rubbery in texture. It is very firm and won't break up during cooking. It is suitable for marinating, stir-frying, pan-frying or barbecuing. It can be processed to use as a base for patties.

Tofu (silken): is very soft and used in soups and sometimes desserts. It holds its shape when cut and cooked if handled carefully.

Tofu (silken firm): *slightly firmer than silken tofu but it holds its shape a little better. It is suitable for dishes such as Agedashi tofu and soups.*

Tom Yum paste: *is used as a base flavour for soups and other dishes. It is made from garlic, chilli, galangal, kaffir lime leaves, lemon grass and shrimp paste. For vegetarian cooking, ensure the brand you buy does not contain shrimp paste or fish sauce.*

Turmeric (fresh and ground): *this spice has a bitter flavour and is best known in its dried powdery form. However, it is also available fresh as a root (similar to fresh ginger). It is also called Indian saffron as it is often used in cooking to colour food. Be careful when handling fresh turmeric as it will stain your hands and clothes.*

Vegetarian oyster sauce: *is made using mushrooms as its flavouring base instead of oysters. With a very similar taste to oyster sauce, this sauce is great for vegetarians.*

Vietnamese mint (also laksa leaf and Cambodia mint): *despite its common name, this trailing herb with narrow, pointed, pungent-tasting leaves doesn't belong to the mint family. Its flavour resembles coriander, but slightly sharper, and is eaten fresh in salads.*

Wakame (curly seaweed): *a type of curly leaf brown algae found in coastal waters, with a soft texture and mild vegetable taste. The whole leaf is blanched and sold undried in Japan or dried and exported. Wakame is used in salads or as a vegetable after boiling for 10 minutes.*

Wasabi paste: *is the edible root of the 'Wasabia japonica' plant which only grows in Japan. The skinned pale-green root has a fierce flavour like horseradish. It is grated or made into a paste and served with sashimi or in sushi. It can be dried to a pale-brown/green powder. Also called Japanese horseradish, mountain hollyhock or wasebi.*

White miso (also shiro miso): *A very light-coloured, almost sweet, miso suitable for making salad dressings. It is a thick fermented paste made from soya beans and other ingredients, including wheat and rice. It is available in other varieties such as light brown, red, brown and yellow, each differing in flavour and texture. It is used in soups, sauces, marinades and dips.*

Won ton wrappers: *are thin squares of dough made from wheat flour and egg yolks. They are mainly used for deep-frying.*

Bamboo mat: made from sticks of bamboo or cane held together by string. Used to help roll up sushi evenly. Available from Asian food stores and some supermarkets.

Bamboo steamers/woven baskets: made from bamboo or cane with close-fitting lids. They are used for steaming various food, such as Chinese dim-sum. Available in different sizes, they can be stacked on top of each other to steam larger quantities.

Chopsticks: are not only used for eating Asian food, but for mixing tempura batter—a tempura batter should be lumpy, and chopsticks make it difficult to mix into a smooth batter. They are also a great tool for holding on to food when dipping into batter.

Draining ladle: with a wooden handle and a woven metal spoon, this ladle is used to lift deep-fried food from the oil and drain off any excess oil. If unavailable, use a slotted spoon.

Draining rack: a metal or wire rack that sits on the rim of a wok, used to drain food that has been deep-fried. Do not leave sitting for too long or the steam from the oil will soften the crisp deep-fried surface. Most commonly used for tempura. If unavailable, drain foods on crumpled paper towel.

Ginger grater: made from wood or ceramic with little grooves to shred the ginger. Is available from Asian food stores and some supermarkets. If unavailable, use a standard grater.

Mortar and pestle: a heavy bowl shape and a heavy short implement with a rounded end used for crushing and grinding foods and spices by hand to a paste or fine powder. Made from granite or marble, it is available in various sizes from Asian stores or kitchenware shops. A spice grinder or food processor can be used instead.

Sharp knives/cleaver: have a set of knives which will allow the right knife for the right job. A cleaver is commonly used in preparing Asian food as it can cut through harder foods than your knives may be able to. It's important to keep your knives sharp—blunt knives make the work so much harder. Cleavers are available from Asian food stores or kitchenware shops.

Wok, charn and wok stand: woks are available in materials such as carbon steel, copper, stainless steel, cast iron and non-stick. A heavy wok will retain the heat better without burning. Electric woks are also available. The wok is used to stir-fry, steam and deep-fry. A **wok stand** is used to hold the wok in place on the stove if you don't have a built-in wok burner. The **charn** is shaped to fit a wok's curves, allowing it to get under the food and stir-fry easily. If using a non-stick wok, use a plastic or wooden charn. These are available from Asian food stores, supermarkets or kitchenware stores.

Asian vegetarian food

Explore the range of meatless possibilities from China to Japan, Thailand to India— a fusion of today's banquet-style cuisines.

Thai spicy sour soup

Preparation time:
  15 minutes
Total cooking time:
  15 minutes
Serves 4–6

3 cups (750 ml)
  vegetable stock
2 tablespoons Tom
  Yum paste (see Note)
2 cm x 2 cm piece
  galangal, peeled and
  cut into thin slices
1 stem lemon grass,
  lightly crushed and
  cut into 4 lengths
3 fresh kaffir lime leaves
1 small red chilli, finely
  sliced on the diagonal
  (optional)
200 g button
  mushrooms, halved
200 g silken firm tofu,
  cut into 1.5 cm cubes
200 g baby bok choy,
  roughly shredded
2 tablespoons lime juice
4 tablespoons fresh
  coriander leaves

1. Place the stock, Tom Yum paste, galangal, lemon grass, kaffir lime leaves, chilli and 3 cups (750 ml) water in a saucepan. Cover and bring to the boil, then reduce the heat and simmer for 5 minutes.
2. Add the mushrooms and tofu and simmer for 5 minutes, or until the mushrooms are tender. Add the bok choy and simmer for a further minute, or until wilted. Remove from the heat and stir in the lime juice and coriander leaves. Serve.

NUTRITION PER SERVE (6)
*Protein 10 g; Fat 1.5 g;
Carbohydrate 1 g; Dietary
Fibre 3.5 g; Cholesterol
0 mg; 763 kJ (180 cal)*

Note: Check the label of the Tom Yum paste to make sure it doesn't contain shrimp paste. If desired, remove the galangal, lemon grass and lime leaves before serving.

Thai spicy sour soup

Miso udon noodle soup

Preparation time:
10 minutes
Total cooking time:
20 minutes
Serves 4

5 g *konbu, cut into*
strips
4 *tablespoons white*
miso paste
2 *tablespoons mirin*
400 g *fresh udon*
noodles
50 g *fresh shiitake*
mushrooms, sliced
2 *spring onions, sliced*

1. Place the konbu and
1.2 litres water in a
saucepan. Bring to the
boil, reduce the heat and
simmer for 10 minutes.
Discard the konbu.
2. Stir in the miso and
mirin over medium
heat. Do not boil or the
liquid will lose flavour.
3. Add the noodles and
cook, without boiling,
for 4–5 minutes, or until
the noodles are tender.
Stir in the mushrooms
for 1 minute. Garnish
with the spring onion.

NUTRITION PER SERVE
Protein 14 g; Fat 1 g;
Carbohydrate 72 g; Dietary
Fibre 4 g; Cholesterol
0 mg; 1530 kJ (365 cal)

Miso udon noodle soup (top)
and Bondas

Bondas

Preparation time:
30 minutes
Total cooking time:
25 minutes
Makes 24

2 *teaspoons oil*
1 *teaspoon brown*
mustard seeds
1 *onion, finely chopped*
2 *teaspoons grated*
fresh ginger
4 *curry leaves*
3 *small green chillies,*
finely chopped
1.2 kg *potatoes, diced*
and cooked
pinch ground turmeric
2 *tablespoons lemon*
juice
4 *tablespoons chopped*
fresh coriander leaves
oil, for deep-frying

Batter
1 *cup (110 g) besan*
flour
1/4 *cup (30 g) self-*
raising flour
1/4 *cup (45 g) rice flour*
1/4 *teaspoon ground*
turmeric
1 *teaspoon chilli*
powder

1. Heat the oil in a
saucepan, add the
mustard seeds and stir
over medium heat for
30 seconds, or until

fragrant. Add the
onion, ginger, curry
leaves and chilli and
cook for 2 minutes. Add
the potato, turmeric
and 2 teaspoons of
water and stir for
2 minutes, or until the
mixture is dry. Remove
from the heat and
cool. Stir in the lemon
juice and coriander
leaves, then season to
taste with salt and
freshly ground black
pepper. Using a heaped
tablespoon, shape into
24 balls.
2. To make the batter,
sift the flours, turmeric,
chilli powder and
1/4 teaspoon salt into
a bowl. Make a well in
the centre of the dry
ingredients. Gradually
whisk in 1 1/3 cups
(330 ml) water to make
a smooth batter.
3. Fill a wok or deep
heavy-based saucepan
one third full of oil and
heat to 180°C (350°F),
or until a cube of bread
dropped into the oil
browns in 15 seconds.
Dip the balls into the
batter, then cook in the
hot oil, in batches, for
1–2 minutes, or until
golden. Drain on paper
towels and season with
salt. Serve hot.

NUTRITION PER BONDA
Protein 1.8 g; Fat 2 g;
Carbohydrate 13 g; Dietary
Fibre 1 g; Cholesterol
0 mg; 333 kJ (80 cal)

Betel rolls

Preparation time:
15 minutes +
10 minutes soaking
Total cooking time:
5 minutes
Makes 24

2 tablespoons sugar
24 betel leaves or large
  fresh basil leaves
1 tablespoon oil
2 cloves garlic, crushed
1 tablespoon grated
  fresh ginger
2 small red chillies,
  seeded and finely
  chopped
200 g fried tofu puffs,
  shredded
2 fresh kaffir lime
  leaves, finely shredded
3 tablespoons lime juice
2 tablespoons shaved
  palm sugar or soft
  brown sugar
3 tablespoons fresh
  coriander leaves
*1/2 cup (45 g) desiccated
  coconut, toasted*

1. Combine the sugar
and 2 cups (500 ml)
water in a bowl. Stir in
the betel leaves, soak for
10 minutes, then drain.
2. Heat the oil in a
frying pan and cook the
garlic, ginger and chilli
over medium heat for
1 minute. Add the tofu,
lime leaves and the
combined juice, palm
sugar and coriander.

Stir until the tofu is
heated through.
3. Place 1 tablespoon of
the tofu mixture onto
each leaf and sprinkle
with coconut. Roll up
the leaves tightly to eat.

NUTRITION PER ROLL
*Protein 1 g; Fat 3 g;
Carbohydrate 4 g; Dietary
Fibre 1 g; Cholesterol
0 mg; 195 kJ (46 cal)*

Note: If using basil
leaves do not soak.

Indonesian peanut fritters

Preparation time:
10 minutes
Total cooking time:
15 minutes
Makes 25

Dipping sauce
1 tablespoon rice
  vinegar
1 tablespoon mirin
2 tablespoons kecap
  manis
*1/4 teaspoon finely
  grated fresh ginger*

1 cup (175 g) rice flour
1 clove garlic, crushed
1 teaspoon ground
  turmeric
*1/2 teaspoon ground
  cumin*
3 teaspoons sambal
  oelek

*1 1/2 teaspoons ground
  coriander*
1 tablespoon finely
  chopped fresh
  coriander leaves
200 ml coconut milk
*1 1/4 cups (200 g)
  roasted unsalted
  peanuts*
oil, for deep-frying

1. To make the dipping
sauce, combine all the
ingredients and cover.
2. To make the fritters,
combine the flour, garlic,
turmeric, cumin, sambal
oelek, ground coriander,
coriander leaves, and
1/2 teaspoon salt in a
bowl. Gradually add
the coconut milk until
the mixture is smooth.
Mix in the peanuts and
50 ml hot water.
3. Fill a wok or deep
heavy-based saucepan
one third full of oil and
heat to 180°C (350°F),
or until a cube of bread
dropped into the oil
browns in 15 seconds.
Cook level tablespoons
of mixture in batches
for 1–2 minutes, or
until golden. Drain
on paper towels and
season. Serve with the
dipping sauce.

NUTRITION PER FRITTER
*Protein 2.5 g; Fat 7.5 g;
Carbohydrate 7 g; Dietary
Fibre 1 g; Cholesterol
0 mg; 440 kJ (105 cal)*

*Betel rolls (top) and
Indonesian peanut fritters*

Using a sharp knife, cut the mango flesh into even matchstick-like strips.

Lift the rice wrapper out of the water when softened.

Fresh rice paper rolls

Preparation time:
40 minutes
Total cooking time:
Nil
Makes 20

Dipping sauce
1/4 cup (60 ml) sweet chilli sauce
1 tablespoon lime juice

100 g dried rice vermicelli
1/2 green mango, julienned
1 small Lebanese cucumber, julienned
1/2 avocado, julienned
4 spring onions, thinly sliced
1/2 cup (15 g) fresh coriander leaves
2 tablespoons chopped fresh Vietnamese mint

1 tablespoon sweet chilli sauce
2 tablespoons lime juice
20 square (15 cm) rice paper wrappers

1. To make the dipping sauce, place the sweet chilli sauce and lime juice in a small bowl and mix together well.
2. To make the rolls, place the vermicelli in a bowl, cover with boiling water and leave for 5 minutes, or until softened. Drain, then cut into short lengths.
3. Place the vermicelli, mango, cucumber, avocado, spring onion, coriander, mint, sweet chilli sauce and lime juice in a bowl and mix together well.
4. Working with no more than two rice paper wrappers at a time, dip each wrapper in a bowl of warm water for 10 seconds to soften, then lay out on a flat work surface. Place 1 tablespoon of the filling on the wrapper, fold in the sides and roll up tightly. Repeat with the remaining filling and rice paper wrappers. Serve the fresh rice paper rolls immediately with the dipping sauce.

NUTRITION PER ROLL
Protein 0 g; Fat 0 g; Carbohydrate 1.3 g; Dietary Fibre 1 g; Cholesterol 0 mg; 53 kJ (13 cal)

Note: Ensure the rice paper rolls are tightly rolled together or they will fall apart while you are eating them. These rolls can be made 2–3 hours ahead of time—layer the rolls in an airtight container between layers of greaseproof paper or plastic wrap, then store in the refrigerator.

Fresh rice paper rolls

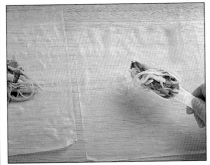

Place 1 tablespoon of the filling into the centre of the wrapper.

Fold in the sides of the wrapper and roll up tightly.

15

Sushi

Preparation time:
  40 minutes +
  15 minutes standing
Total cooking time:
  20 minutes
Makes 30

7 nori sheets
30 g carrot, julienned
50 g potato, julienned
30 g zucchini, grated
50 g onion, finely sliced
40 g orange sweet
  potato, grated
3 spring onions,
  green part included,
  cut into 2 cm lengths
1 cup (125 g) tempura
  flour
1 cup (250 ml) chilled
  soda water
oil, for deep-frying
2 cups (440 g) short-
  grain white rice
2 tablespoons rice
  vinegar
2 tablespoons caster
  sugar
wasabi paste, to taste
2 tablespoons shredded
  pickled ginger

1. Shred 2 nori sheets and place in a bowl. Add the carrot, potato, zucchini, onion, orange sweet potato and spring onion and mix together.
2. Sift the tempura flour into a large bowl and make a well in the centre. Add the soda water and loosely mix in with chopsticks or a fork until the ingredients are just combined—the batter should still be a little lumpy. Add the vegetable mixture to the batter and quickly fold through.
3. Fill a wok or deep heavy-based saucepan one third full of oil and heat to 180°C (350°F), or until a cube of bread dropped into the oil browns in 15 seconds.
4. Gently drop 1/4 cup (60 ml) of the mixture into the oil, making sure that the patty is not too compact, and cook for 1–2 minutes, or until golden. Drain on crumpled paper towels, season with salt and repeat with the remaining mixture to make five patties.
5. To make the vinegar rice, rinse the rice under running water until the water runs clear. Put the rice and 2 cups (500 ml) water in a saucepan, bring slowly to the boil, then reduce the heat and simmer gently for 10 minutes. Remove from the heat and set aside, covered, for 15 minutes.
6. Spread the rice out in a shallow dish. Put the vinegar, sugar, 1/2 teaspoon salt and 1 tablespoon water in a small saucepan and stir over low heat until both the sugar and salt have dissolved. Gently pour the liquid over the rice, fork it through and leave to cool.
7. Place one of the remaining nori sheets, shiny-side down, on a bamboo mat or a sheet of non-stick baking paper with a short end towards you. Spread one fifth of the rice over the bottom third of the nori sheet, leaving a 2 cm border. Spread a thin layer of wasabi paste in a line down the centre of the rice. Break up a vegetable patty and arrange over the wasabi paste. Top with one fifth of the pickled ginger and, using the mat or paper as a guide, firmly roll up the nori sheet to enclose the filling. Using a sharp knife, cut the sushi roll in half, then each half into three slices, wiping the knife between slices. Repeat with the remaining filling and nori sheets.

NUTRITION PER SUSHI
Protein 10 g; Fat 1 g;
Carbohydrate 127 g; Dietary
Fibre 4.5 g; Cholesterol
0 mg; 2719 kJ (650 cal)

Sushi

Asian noodle soup

Preparation time:
20 minutes +
20 minutes soaking
Total cooking time:
15 minutes
Serves 4

8 dried Chinese
mushrooms
100 g dried rice
vermicelli
800 g Chinese broccoli,
cut into 5 cm lengths
8 fried tofu puffs,
cut into strips
125 g bean sprouts
1 litre vegetable stock
2 tablespoons light soy
sauce
1½ tablespoons
Chinese rice wine
3 spring onions, finely
chopped
fresh purple basil
leaves, to serve

1. Place the mushrooms in a bowl, cover with boiling water and soak for 15 minutes. Drain, reserving ½ cup (125 ml) of the liquid. Squeeze the mushrooms to remove any excess liquid. Discard the stems and thinly slice the caps.
2. Soak the vermicelli in boiling water for 5 minutes. Drain.

Divide the vermicelli, broccoli, tofu puffs and bean sprouts among the four serving bowls.
3. Place the reserved mushroom liquid, stock, soy sauce, wine, spring onion and mushrooms in a saucepan and bring to the boil. Cook, covered, for 10 minutes.
4. Ladle the soup into the serving bowls and garnish with the fresh basil leaves. Serve.

NUTRITION PER SERVE
Protein 17 g; Fat 6.5 g; Carbohydrate 12 g; Dietary Fibre 13 g; Cholesterol 0 mg; 757 kJ (180 cal)

Laksa

Preparation time:
25 minutes
Total cooking time:
10 minutes
Serves 4

200 g dried rice
vermicelli
2 tablespoons peanut
oil
2–3 tablespoons laksa
paste (see Note)
1 litre vegetable stock
3 cups (750 ml)
coconut milk
250 g snow peas,
halved diagonally
5 spring onions,
cut into 3 cm lengths

2 tablespoons lime juice
125 g bean sprouts
200 g fried tofu puffs,
halved
3 tablespoons roughly
chopped fresh
Vietnamese mint
⅔ cup (20 g) fresh
coriander leaves

1. Place the vermicelli in a large bowl, cover with boiling water and soak for 5 minutes.
2. Heat the oil in a large saucepan, add the laksa paste and cook, stirring, over medium heat for 1 minute, or until fragrant. Add the stock, coconut milk, snow peas and spring onion and simmer for 5 minutes. Pour in the lime juice and season to taste with salt and freshly ground black pepper.
3. Drain the vermicelli and divide among four bowls. Top with the bean sprouts and fried tofu puffs. Ladle the hot soup into the serving bowls and sprinkle with the fresh mint and coriander. Serve immediately.

NUTRITION PER SERVE
Protein 14 g; Fat 55 g; Carbohydrate 30 g; Dietary Fibre 12 g; Cholesterol 1 mg; 2780 kJ (665 cal)

Note: Ensure the laksa paste doesn't contain shrimp paste.

Asian noodle soup (top) and Laksa

Nori cones

Preparation time:
  45 minutes +
  15 minutes standing +
  5 minutes soaking
Total cooking time:
  15 minutes
Makes 40

2 cups (440 g) short-
  grain white rice
2 tablespoons rice
  vinegar
2 tablespoons caster
  sugar
10 g sliced dried
  Chinese mushrooms
250 g choy sum,
  shredded and
  blanched
1 tablespoon pickled
  ginger, shredded
1 tablespoon toasted
  sesame seeds
1 tablespoon kecap
  manis
1/2 teaspoon wasabi
  paste
2 teaspoons mirin

*1 tablespoon salt-
  reduced soy sauce*
10 nori sheets
*purchased dipping sauce
  for sushi, to serve*

1. Rinse the rice until
the water runs clear.
Put in a saucepan with
2 cups (500 ml) water.
Bring to the boil, then
reduce the heat and
simmer for 10 minutes.
Remove from the heat,
cover and stand for
15 minutes.
2. Spread the rice out
in a shallow dish. Place
the vinegar, sugar,
1/2 teaspoon salt and
2 tablespoons water in
a saucepan and stir
over low heat until the
sugar and salt have
dissolved. Pour over
the rice, fork it through
and cool.
3. Soak the mushrooms
in boiling water for
5 minutes. Drain,

squeeze out the excess
liquid and roughly chop.
4. Place the rice in a
large bowl and stir in
the mushrooms, choy
sum, ginger, sesame
seeds and the combined
kecap manis, wasabi,
mirin and soy sauce.
5. Place the nori sheets
shiny-side down and
cut each sheet into four
squares. Brush the
joining edge with water
and place 1 tablespoon
of the mixture in the
centre of the square.
Roll up on the diagonal
to form a cone and top
up with 2 teaspoons of
filling. Repeat with the
remaining filling and
nori sheets. Serve
immediately with the
sushi dipping sauce.

NUTRITION PER CONE
*Protein 1.5 g; Fat 0 g;
Carbohydrate 20 g; Dietary
Fibre 0.8 g; Cholesterol
0 mg; 392 kJ (93 cal)*

Nori cones

*Pour the vinegar, sugar, salt and water
mixture evenly over the rice.*

*Using kitchen scissors, cut each nori sheet
into four squares.*

Roll the sheets on the diagonal to form a cone.

Top up each cone with an extra 2 teaspoons of the filling mixture.

21

Split pea and vegetable soup

Preparation time:
10 minutes
Total cooking time:
1 hour 10 minutes
Serves 4

1 tablespoon peanut or
 vegetable oil
1 onion, chopped
2 cloves garlic, chopped
1¹/2 teaspoons chopped
 fresh ginger
1¹/2 tablespoons
 Madras curry paste
100 g yellow split peas,
 rinsed and drained
1 large zucchini, peeled
 and chopped
1 large carrot, roughly
 chopped
170 g button
 mushrooms, roughly
 chopped
1 celery stick, roughly
 chopped
1 litre vegetable stock
¹/2 cup (125 ml) cream

1. Heat the oil in a
saucepan, add the
onion and cook over
low heat for 5 minutes,
or until soft. Add the
garlic, ginger and curry
paste and cook over
medium heat for
2 minutes. Stir in the
split peas until well
coated with paste, then
add the vegetables and
cook for 2 minutes.
2. Add the stock, bring
to the boil, then reduce
the heat and simmer,
partly covered, for
1 hour. Remove from
the heat and allow to
cool slightly.
3. Transfer to a blender
or food processor and
process the soup in
batches until smooth.
Return to the pan, stir
in the cream and gently
heat until warmed
through. Serve with
naan bread, if desired.

NUTRITION PER SERVE
*Protein 9.5 g; Fat 20 g;
Carbohydrate 18 g; Dietary
Fibre 6 g; Cholesterol
43 mg; 1199 kJ (287 cal)*

Spiced chickpea and vegetable soup

Preparation time:
10 minutes
Total cooking time:
30 minutes
Serves 4–6

1 tablespoon peanut oil
1 onion, chopped
2 cloves garlic, crushed
1 celery stick, roughly
 chopped
1 large carrot, roughly
 chopped
1 large potato, roughly
 chopped
1–2 teaspoons Madras
 curry powder,
 or to taste
1 teaspoon ground
 cumin
1 tablespoon tomato
 paste
410 g can chickpeas,
 drained
1.5 litres vegetable
 stock
1 cup (155 g) frozen
 peas
2 tablespoons chopped
 fresh coriander leaves

1. Heat the oil in a
large saucepan. Add
the onion and garlic
and cook over medium
heat for 1–2 minutes,
or until the onion is
soft. Add the celery,
carrot, potato, curry
powder and cumin
and cook for a further
2 minutes.
2. Stir in the tomato
paste, chickpeas and
stock. Bring to the
boil, then reduce the
heat and simmer for
20 minutes, or until
reduced slightly.
Stir in the peas and
coriander and cook
for 2–3 minutes, or
until warmed through.
Season to taste with
salt and freshly ground
black pepper. Serve
immediately.

NUTRITION PER SERVE (6)
*Protein 15 g; Fat 7.5 g;
Carbohydrate 33 g; Dietary
Fibre 12 g; Cholesterol
0 mg; 1083 kJ (260 cal)*

---

*Split pea and vegetable soup (top)
and Spiced chickpea and vegetable soup*

Thai sweet potato soup

Preparation time:
10 minutes
Total cooking time:
40 minutes
Serves 4–6

1 tablespoon peanut oil
2 onions, chopped
2 cloves garlic, chopped
2 teaspoons cumin
seeds
1 small red chilli,
roughly chopped
1.5 kg orange sweet
potato, roughly
chopped
1.5 litres vegetable
stock
275 ml coconut milk
fresh coriander leaves,
to garnish

1. Heat the oil in a
large saucepan, add the
onion and cook for
1–2 minutes, or until
softened. Stir in the
garlic, cumin and chilli
and cook for 2 minutes.
Add the sweet potato
and cook for 2 minutes.
2. Add the stock, bring
to the boil, then reduce
the heat and simmer,
partly covered, for
30 minutes, or until
the sweet potato is
tender. Cool slightly.
3. Transfer to a blender
or food processor and
blend in batches until
smooth. Return to the
heat, stir in the coconut
milk until warmed.
Serve garnished with
coriander leaves.

NUTRITION PER SERVE (6)
*Protein 5.5 g; Fat 13 g;
Carbohydrate 46 g; Dietary
Fibre 6.3 g; Cholesterol
0 mg; 1335 kJ (320 cal)*

Samosas

Preparation time:
30 minutes
Total cooking time:
25 minutes
Makes 24

1 tablespoon oil
1 onion, chopped
1 teaspoon grated
fresh ginger
1 clove garlic, crushed
2 teaspoons ground
coriander
2 teaspoons ground
cumin
2 teaspoons garam
masala
1$\frac{1}{2}$ teaspoons chilli
powder
$\frac{1}{4}$ teaspoon ground
turmeric
300 g potatoes, cut into
1 cm cubes and boiled
$\frac{1}{4}$ cup (40 g) frozen
peas
2 tablespoons chopped
fresh coriander leaves
1 teaspoon lemon juice
6 sheets ready-rolled
puff pastry
oil, for deep-frying

1. Heat the oil in a
saucepan. Add the
onion, ginger and garlic
and cook over medium
heat for 2 minutes, or
until soft. Add the
spices, potato, peas and
2 teaspoons water.
Cook for 1 minute, or
until all the moisture
evaporates. Remove
from the heat and stir
in the coriander leaves
and lemon juice.
2. Cut 12 rounds from
the pastry sheets with
a 12.5 cm cutter, then
cut each round in half.
Shape 1 semi-circle into
a cone, wet the edges
and seal the side seam,
leaving an opening
large enough to spoon
in 3 teaspoons of filling,
then seal. Repeat with
the remaining pastry
and filling.
3. Fill a wok or deep
heavy-based saucepan
one third full of oil and
heat to 180°C (350°F),
or until a cube of bread
dropped into the oil
browns in 15 seconds.
Cook in batches for
1–2 minutes, or until
golden. Drain on paper
towels and season.
Serve hot with yoghurt.

NUTRITION PER SAMOSA
*Protein 2 g; Fat 8.5 g;
Carbohydrate 12 g; Dietary
Fibre 1 g; Cholesterol
7 mg; 560 kJ (135 cal)*

*Thai sweet potato soup (top)
and Samosas*

Steamed tofu with soy

Preparation time:
15 minutes +
30 minutes marinating
Total cooking time:
7 minutes
Serves 4

1 teaspoon sesame oil
2 tablespoons soy sauce
2 tablespoons kecap
   manis
500 g firm tofu, drained
1¹/2 teaspoons
   julienned fresh ginger
3 spring onions, finely
   sliced on the diagonal
1 cup (50 g) chopped
   fresh coriander leaves
1–2 tablespoons
   purchased fried garlic
   or fried shallots,
   to garnish

1. Combine the oil, soy sauce and kecap manis in a bowl. Cut the tofu in half widthways, then into triangles. Place on a plate and pour on the sauce. Marinate for 30 minutes, turning the tofu once.
2. Sprinkle the ginger over the tofu. Place the plate on a wire rack over a wok or saucepan of simmering water. Cover and steam for 3–4 minutes. Sprinkle with the spring onion and coriander, then cover and steam for 3 minutes. Garnish with the fried garlic.

NUTRITION PER SERVE
Protein 5 g; Fat 3.3 g;
Carbohydrate 1 g; Dietary
Fibre 0 g; Cholesterol
0 mg; 231 kJ (55 cal)

Tofu with chilli relish and cashews

Preparation time:
20 minutes
Total cooking time:
30 minutes
Serves 4

Chilli relish
¹/3 cup (80 ml) peanut
   oil
12 red Asian shallots,
   chopped
8 cloves garlic, chopped
8 fresh long red chillies,
   chopped
2 red capsicums,
   chopped
1 tablespoon tamarind
   concentrate
1 tablespoon soy sauce
100 g palm sugar, grated

2 tablespoons kecap
   manis
1 tablespoon peanut oil
6 spring onions,
   cut into 3 cm lengths
750 g silken firm tofu,
   cut into 3 cm cubes

3/4 cup (25 g) fresh
   Thai basil
2/3 cup (100 g) roasted
   salted cashews

1. To make the relish, heat half the oil in a frying pan. Add the shallots and garlic and cook over medium heat for 2 minutes. Transfer to a food processor, add the chilli and capsicum and process until smooth. Heat the remaining oil in the pan, add the shallot mixture and cook over medium heat for 2 minutes. Stir in the tamarind, soy sauce and sugar and cook for 20 minutes.
2. Place 2–3 tablespoons of the relish with the kecap manis in a bowl and mix. Heat the oil in a wok over high heat and swirl to coat. Add the spring onion and cook for 30 seconds. Remove. Add the tofu, stir-fry for 1 minute, then add the relish and kecap manis mixture. Cook for 3 minutes, or until the tofu is coated and heated through. Return the spring onion to the wok, add the basil and cashews and cook until the basil has wilted.

NUTRITION PER SERVE
Protein 16 g; Fat 37 g;
Carbohydrate 38 g; Dietary
Fibre 4 g; Cholesterol
0 mg; 2533 kJ (605 cal)

Steamed tofu with soy (top) and
Tofu with chilli relish and cashews

Sticky rice pockets

Preparation time:
1 hour +
10 minutes soaking
Total cooking time:
2 hours
Makes 20

20 dried bamboo leaves
1/2 cup (125 ml) oil
6 spring onions,
    chopped
400 g eggplant,
    cut into 1 cm cubes
1/2 cup (90 g) drained
    water chestnuts,
    chopped
1 tablespoon
    mushroom soy sauce
3 small red chillies,
    seeded and finely
    chopped
2 teaspoons sugar
3 tablespoons chopped
    fresh coriander leaves
4 cups (800 g) white
    glutinous rice, washed
    and well drained
2 tablespoons soy sauce

1. Soak the bamboo leaves in boiling water for 10 minutes, or until soft. Drain.
2. Heat half the oil in a wok. Cook the spring onion and eggplant over high heat for 4–5 minutes, or until golden. Stir in the water chestnuts, soy sauce, chilli, sugar and coriander. Cool.
3. Bring 3 cups (750 ml) water to a simmer. Heat the remaining oil in a saucepan, add the rice and stir for 2 minutes, or until coated. Stir in 1/2 cup (125 ml) of the hot water over low heat until it is all absorbed. Repeat until all the water has been added (about 20 minutes). Add the soy sauce and season with white pepper.
4. Fold one end of a bamboo leaf on the diagonal to form a cone. Hold securely in one hand and spoon in 2 tablespoons of rice. Make an indent in the rice, add 1 tablespoon eggplant filling, then top with 1 tablespoon of rice. Fold the other end of the bamboo leaf over to enclose the filling, then secure with a toothpick. Tie tightly with string. Repeat with the remaining bamboo leaves, rice and filling.
5. Place in a single layer inside a double bamboo steamer. Cover and place over a wok half filled with simmering water. Steam for 1 hour 30 minutes, or until the rice is tender, adding more boiling water as needed. Serve hot.

NUTRITION PER POCKET
*Protein 1.5 g; Fat 6 g;
Carbohydrate 13 g; Dietary
Fibre 1 g; Cholesterol
0 mg; 465 kJ (111 cal)*

Sticky rice pockets

Stir-fry the vegetables, soy sauce and coriander over high heat.

Fold one end of the bamboo leaf over on the diagonal to form a cone shape.

Spoon 2 tablespoons of the rice mixture into each cone.

Fold over the excess bamboo leaf to totally enclose the filling.

Dhal

Preparation time:
10 minutes
Total cooking time:
40 minutes
Serves 6

1 cup (250 g) red lentils
1/4 teaspoon ground
    turmeric
1 tablespoon oil
1/2 teaspoon brown
    mustard seeds
1 tablespoon cumin
    seeds
1 onion, finely chopped
1 tablespoon grated
    fresh ginger
2 long green chillies,
    halved lengthways
1/3 cup (80 ml) lemon
    juice
2 tablespoons finely
    chopped fresh
    coriander leaves

1. Place the lentils in a
saucepan, cover with
3 cups (750 ml) water
and bring to the boil.
Reduce the heat, stir
in the turmeric, then
simmer, covered, for
20 minutes, or until
the lentils are tender.
2. Heat the oil in a
saucepan, add the
mustard and cumin
seeds and cook until
the mustard seeds begin
to pop. Add the onion,
ginger and chilli. Cook
for 5 minutes, or until
the onion is golden.
3. Add the lentils and
1/2 cup (125 ml) water.
Season with salt, reduce
the heat and simmer for
10 minutes. Remove
from the heat, stir in the
lemon juice and garnish
with the coriander.

NUTRITION PER SERVE
Protein 10 g; Fat 4 g;
Carbohydrate 16 g; Dietary
Fibre 6 g; Cholesterol
0 mg; 611 kJ (145 cal)

Mini Thai
spring rolls

Preparation time:
30 minutes +
5 minutes soaking
Total cooking time:
20 minutes
Makes 40

Filling
80 g dried rice
    vermicelli
2 cloves garlic, crushed
1 carrot, grated
4 spring onions, finely
    chopped
1 tablespoon sweet
    chilli sauce
2 teaspoons grated
    fresh ginger
2 fresh coriander roots,
    finely chopped
1 1/2 tablespoons lime
    juice
1 teaspoon shaved
    palm sugar
2 tablespoons chopped
    fresh coriander leaves
3 teaspoons sesame oil
1 tablespoon kecap
    manis

40 square (12.5 cm)
    spring roll wrappers
oil, for deep-frying

1. To make the filling,
soak the vermicelli
in boiling water for
5 minutes. Drain and
cut into short lengths.
Mix with the remaining
filling ingredients.
2. Working with one
wrapper at a time,
spoon 1 tablespoon
of the filling onto
one corner (on the
diagonal), brush the
edges with water and
roll up diagonally,
tucking in the edges as
you go. Repeat with
the remaining filling
and wrappers.
3. Fill a wok or deep
heavy-based saucepan
one third full of oil and
heat to 180°C (350°F),
or until a cube of bread
browns in 15 seconds.
Cook in batches for
2–3 minutes, or until
golden brown. Drain
on paper towels. Serve
with sweet chilli sauce.

NUTRITION PER ROLL
Protein 0 g; Fat 1.3 g;
Carbohydrate 1 g; Dietary
Fibre 0 g; Cholesterol
0 mg; 65 kJ (16 cal)

Dhal (top) and
Mini Thai spring rolls

Agedashi tofu

Preparation time:
15 minutes +
1 hour soaking
Total cooking time:
15 minutes
Serves 4

40 g konbu
1–2 tablespoons soy
  sauce
2–3 teaspoons sugar
2 x 300 g packets
  silken firm tofu
oil, for deep-frying
potato flour, for dusting
4 spring onions, finely
  sliced on the diagonal
20 g daikon, grated
1 teaspoon grated fresh
  ginger

1. Wipe the konbu clean with a damp cloth (do not wash). Place in a large bowl, cover with 1 litre water and leave for 1 hour. Transfer to a saucepan, bring to the boil, but remove from the heat just before boiling point. Discard the konbu. Stir in the soy sauce and sugar, cover and keep hot.
2. Cut the tofu into 3 cm cubes and drain.
3. Fill a wok or deep heavy-based saucepan one third full of oil and heat to 190°C (375°F), or until a cube of bread dropped into the oil browns in 10 seconds.

Gently dust the flour over the tofu, shaking off any excess. Deep-fry in three batches for 2–3 minutes, or until golden, turning halfway through if needed. Drain on paper towels and sprinkle with salt.
4. Ladle 1/2 cup (125 ml) hot broth into each serving bowl and top with the tofu. Sprinkle with the spring onion, daikon and ginger.

NUTRITION PER SERVE
Protein 4 g; Fat 10.5 g; Carbohydrate 3.5 g; Dietary Fibre 0 g; Cholesterol 0 mg; 720 kJ (170 cal)

Rava upma

Preparation time:
10 minutes
Total cooking time:
20 minutes
Serves 6

1 tablespoon oil
1/4 teaspoon brown
  mustard seeds
1/4 cup (40 g) cashews,
  roughly chopped
1 onion, finely chopped
1 teaspoon grated fresh
  ginger
5 dried curry leaves,
  finely chopped
1 small red capsicum,
  finely chopped
1 carrot, finely chopped

pinch ground turmeric
1 1/2 cups (185 g)
  semolina
30 g butter

1. Heat the oil in a saucepan, add the mustard seeds and cook, stirring, over medium heat for 30 seconds, or until the seeds start to pop. Add the cashews and cook for 2 minutes, or until golden. Add the onion, ginger, curry leaves, capsicum and carrot. Cook over low heat for 5 minutes, or until the onion is soft.
2. Stir in the turmeric and 2 1/2 cups (625 ml) water. Season. Bring to the boil, then reduce the heat to low and slowly stir in the semolina, stirring well to prevent lumps. Simmer for 10 minutes, or until the semolina is cooked and any excess moisture has evaporated. Stir in the butter. Serve hot with yoghurt and chutney.

NUTRITION PER SERVE
Protein 5 g; Fat 11 g; Carbohydrate 24 g; Dietary Fibre 2 g; Cholesterol 13 mg; 900 kJ (215 cal)

Note: Curry leaves are small and pointed leaves with a spicy fragrance, available from Asian food stores.

*Agedashi tofu (top)
and Rava upma*

Stir-fry sauces

The following sauces are suitable for many different vegetable combinations. To make the stir-fry for 4 people, cook 500 g vegetables, add the sauce and bring to the boil until thickened.

Sake sauce

Soak 10 g sliced dried Chinese mushrooms in boiling water for 5 minutes. Drain and reserve 2 tablespoons of the liquid. Place 2 tablespoons sake, 2 tablespoons kecap manis, 1 tablespoon sweet chilli sauce, $1/2$ teaspoon sesame oil, 1 small finely chopped red chilli, 2 teaspoons finely chopped lemon grass, 1 tablespoon lime juice, the mushrooms and the reserved liquid in a bowl and stir well. **Serving suggestion:** Mixed vegetables.

Chilli oyster sauce

Place 1 teaspoon sesame oil, 2 cloves crushed garlic, 1 tablespoon grated fresh ginger, 2 finely chopped small red chillies, 4 sliced spring onions, 2 tablespoons mirin and $1/2$ cup (125 ml) vegetable oyster sauce in a bowl and stir together well. **Serving suggestion:** Tempeh, Asian greens and roasted cashews.

Japanese dressing

Place 10 dried shiitake mushrooms in a bowl and cover with $1^{1}/2$ cups (375 ml) boiling water. Soak for 10 minutes. Drain, reserving $1/4$ cup (60 ml) of the liquid and cut the mushrooms in quarters. Place $1/3$ cup (80 ml) Japanese soy sauce, 1 teaspoon grated fresh ginger, $1/3$ cup (80 ml) mirin, 2 tablespoons sugar and the reserved liquid in a bowl. Add the mushrooms and stir together well. **Serving suggestion:** Mixed vegetables and tofu.

Hoisin sauce

Place $1/4$ cup (60 ml) hoisin sauce, 2 tablespoons vegetable stock, 1 tablespoon vegetable oyster sauce and 1 tablespoon sweet chilli sauce in a small bowl and stir together. **Serving suggestion:** Mixed vegetables.

Black bean sauce

Place 2 teaspoons cornflour and $1/2$ cup (125 ml) vegetable stock in a small bowl and blend together. Drain and rinse a 170 g can black beans, place in a bowl and lightly mash with a fork. Stir in the cornflour mixture, 1 tablespoon mushroom soy sauce, 2 teaspoons sugar and 2 cloves crushed garlic. **Serving suggestion:** Mixed vegetables.

Ginger oyster sauce

Combine 2 teaspoons cornflour and 2 teaspoons water. Add $1/2$ cup (125 ml) dry sherry, 1 chopped small red chilli, 1 tablespoon grated fresh ginger, $1/2$ teaspoon sesame oil and 2 tablespoons vegetable oyster sauce and stir well. **Serving suggestion:** Hokkien noodles, mushrooms and mixed Asian greens.

Clockwise from top left: Sake sauce, Chilli oyster sauce, Hoisin sauce, Ginger oyster sauce, Black bean sauce and Japanese dressing.

Braised bok choy

Preparation time:
  10 minutes
Total cooking time:
  5 minutes
Serves 4

2 tablespoons oil
1 clove garlic, crushed
1 tablespoon shredded
  fresh ginger
550 g bok choy,
  cut into 8 cm lengths
1 teaspoon sugar
1 teaspoon sesame oil
1 tablespoon vegetable
  oyster sauce

1. Heat a wok until
very hot, add the oil
and swirl to coat. Add
the garlic and ginger
and stir-fry for
1 minute, then add
the bok choy and stir-
fry for 1 minute. Add
the sugar and 1/4 cup
(60 ml) water. Bring to
the boil, then reduce
the heat and simmer,
covered, for 3 minutes,
or until the stems are
tender but crisp.
2. Stir in the sesame oil
and oyster sauce and
serve immediately.

NUTRITION PER SERVE
*Protein 6.5 g; Fat 11 g;
Carbohydrate 3 g; Dietary
Fibre 6 g; Cholesterol
0 mg; 586 kJ (140 cal)*

---

*Braised bok choy (top)
and Gado gado*

Gado gado

Preparation time:
  30 minutes
Total cooking time:
  30 minutes
Serves 4

2 small carrots,
  thinly sliced
100 g cauliflower,
  cut into small florets
60 g snow peas,
  trimmed
100 g bean sprouts
8 well-shaped iceberg
  lettuce leaves
4 small potatoes,
  cooked and cut into
  thin slices
1 Lebanese cucumber,
  thinly sliced
2 hard-boiled eggs,
  peeled and cut into
  quarters
2 ripe tomatoes,
  cut into wedges

Peanut sauce
1 tablespoon oil
1 small onion, finely
  chopped
1/2 cup (125 g) crunchy
  peanut butter
3/4 cup (185 ml)
  coconut milk
1 teaspoon sambal
  oelek
1 tablespoon lemon
  juice
1 tablespoon kecap
  manis

1. Steam the carrots
and cauliflower in a
saucepan for 5 minutes,
or until nearly tender.
Add the snow peas and
cook for 2 minutes.
Add the bean sprouts
and cook for a further
1 minute. Remove from
the heat and cool.
2. To make the peanut
sauce, heat the oil in a
saucepan and cook the
onion for 5 minutes
over low heat, or until
soft and lightly golden.
Add the peanut butter,
coconut milk, sambal
oelek, lemon juice,
kecap manis and
1/4 cup (60 ml) water,
and stir well. Bring
to the boil, stirring
constantly, then reduce
the heat and simmer for
5 minutes, or until the
sauce has reduced and
thickened. Remove
from the heat.
3. Place two lettuce
leaves together (one
inside the other) to
make 4 lettuce cups.
4. In each lettuce cup,
arrange one quarter
of the potato, carrot,
cauliflower, snow peas,
bean sprouts and
cucumber. Top with
some of the peanut
sauce, and garnish with
the egg and tomato.

NUTRITION PER SERVE
*Protein 18 g; Fat 33 g;
Carbohydrate 20 g; Dietary
Fibre 10 g; Cholesterol
103 mg; 1860 kJ (444 cal)*

Soba noodle salad

Preparation time:
  20 minutes
Total cooking time:
  5 minutes
Serves 4 as an entrée

220 g dried soba noodles
1 small Lebanese
  cucumber
250 g baby bok choy,
  leaves separated and
  blanched
1 red capsicum,
  cut into thin strips
2 teaspoons Japanese
  soy sauce
1 teaspoon sesame oil
1/3 cup (80 ml) mirin
1 teaspoon grated fresh
  ginger
2 teaspoons black
  sesame seeds

1. Cook the noodles in
a saucepan of boiling
water for 1–2 minutes,
or until just tender.
Rinse and drain.
2. Slice the cucumber
into ribbons using a
vegetable peeler and
place in a bowl with
the noodles, bok choy
and capsicum. Stir in
the combined soy sauce,
sesame oil, mirin and
ginger and sprinkle
with sesame seeds.

NUTRITION PER SERVE
*Protein 5 g; Fat 2 g;
Carbohydrate 13 g; Dietary
Fibre 3.5 g; Cholesterol
0 mg; 390 kJ (93 cal)*

Thai tempeh

Preparation time:
  15 minutes +
  overnight marinating
Total cooking time:
  15 minutes
Serves 4

2 stems lemon grass,
  white part only, finely
  chopped
2 fresh kaffir lime
  leaves, shredded
2 small red chillies,
  seeded and finely
  chopped
3 cloves garlic, crushed
2 teaspoons sesame
  oil
1/2 cup (125 ml) lime
  juice
2 teaspoons shaved
  palm sugar
1/2 cup (125 ml) soy
  sauce
600 g tempeh, cut into
  5 mm slices
1/3 cup (80 ml) peanut
  oil
1 tablespoon shaved
  palm sugar, extra
100 g snow pea sprouts
finely shredded fresh
  kaffir lime leaves,
  extra

1. Place the lemon
grass, lime leaves, chilli,
garlic, sesame oil, lime
juice, sugar and soy
sauce in a non-metallic

bowl and mix together
well. Add the tempeh
and stir. Cover with
plastic wrap and
marinate overnight in
the refrigerator, stirring
occasionally. Drain and
reserve the marinade.
2. Heat half the peanut
oil in a frying pan. Add
the tempeh and cook
over high heat in
batches, turning once,
for 5 minutes, or until
crispy. Add more of
the oil when necessary.
Drain on paper towels.
3. Place the reserved
marinade and the extra
sugar in a saucepan and
stir over medium heat.
Bring to the boil and
cook for 3–4 minutes,
or until syrupy.
4. Divide one third of
the tempeh among
the four serving plates
and top with half the
snow pea sprouts. Add
another layer of tempeh
and the remaining
sprouts, then top with
the remaining layer of
tempeh. Drizzle the
marinade syrup over
the top, then sprinkle
with the extra lime
leaves. Serve with Asian
greens, if desired.

NUTRITION PER SERVE
*Protein 2.5 g; Fat 22 g;
Carbohydrate 10 g; Dietary
Fibre 1 g; Cholesterol
0 mg; 1030 kJ (245 cal)*

*Soba noodle salad (top)
and Thai tempeh*

Vegetable koftas with tomato sauce

Preparation time:
  30 minutes
Total cooking time:
  25 minutes
Makes 20

180 g cauliflower,
  roughly chopped
180 g cabbage, chopped
1 large zucchini, diced
1 large carrot, chopped
1¹/4 cups (155 g) plain
  flour
1 teaspoon garam
  masala
1 teaspoon ground
  cumin
¹/2 teaspoon ground
  coriander
oil, for deep-frying

Tomato sauce
1 onion, chopped
2 cloves garlic
2 cm x 2 cm piece
  ginger, peeled and
  chopped
1 green chilli, chopped
2 tablespoons shredded
  coconut
1 teaspoon cumin seeds
1 tablespoon oil
¹/4 teaspoon chilli
  powder
400 g puréed tomatoes
1 cup (250 ml) cream

1. Place the vegetables
in a food processor in
batches and process
until finely chopped.
Transfer the mixture
to a bowl and stir in
the flour and spices.
Form the mixture into
20 golf ball-sized balls.
2. Fill a wok or deep
heavy-based saucepan
one third full of oil and
heat to 180°C (350°F),
or until a cube of bread
dropped into the oil
browns in 15 seconds.
Cook the koftas in
batches for 2 minutes,
or until golden. Drain.
3. To make the sauce,
place the onion, garlic,
ginger, chilli, coconut
and cumin in a food
processor and process
until it forms a paste.
4. Heat the oil in a
saucepan, add the paste
and chilli powder and
cook over medium heat
for 3–4 minutes, or
until fragrant. Add the
tomato and bring to
the boil. Reduce the
heat and simmer for
5 minutes. Stir in the
cream and simmer for
a further 5 minutes.
Serve the koftas with
a drizzle of sauce.
Garnish with coriander
leaves, if desired.

NUTRITION PER KOFTA
*Protein 2 g; Fat 9 g;
Carbohydrate 8 g; Dietary
Fibre 2 g; Cholesterol
17 mg; 500 kJ (120 cal)*

Asian greens with roasted cashews

Preparation time:
  10 minutes
Total cooking time:
  5 minutes
Serves 4

300 g broccoli,
  cut into florets
500 g baby bok choy,
  leaves separated
150 g snow peas
155 g asparagus spears,
  cut in half diagonally
1 tablespoon peanut oil
2 teaspoons sesame oil
2 tablespoons kecap
  manis
2 teaspoons mushroom
  soy sauce
¹/4 cup (40 g) roasted
  cashews
¹/4 teaspoon sesame
  seeds

1. Steam the vegetables
for 3–4 minutes, or
until just tender.
2. Heat the oils in a
small saucepan. Add
the sauces and cook,
stirring, over medium
heat for 1 minute, or
until heated through.
Add the sauce to the
vegetables and toss.
Sprinkle with the nuts
and sesame seeds.

NUTRITION PER SERVE
*Protein 15 g; Fat 15 g;
Carbohydrate 8 g; Dietary
Fibre 12 g; Cholesterol
0 mg; 950 kJ (227 cal)*

*Vegetables kofta with tomato sauce (top)
and Asian greens with roasted cashews*

Tofu balls with salad

Preparation time:
20 minutes
Total cooking time:
10 minutes
Serves 4

Salad dressing
3 cloves garlic, chopped
*1/2 cup (80 g) roasted
unsalted peanuts*
2 tablespoons tamari
*1/3 cup (80 ml) lime
juice*
2 tablespoons soft
brown sugar

300 g hard tofu,
roughly chopped
1 tablespoon chopped
fresh garlic chives
2 tablespoons sweet
chilli sauce
2 fresh kaffir lime
leaves, finely shredded
1 stem lemon grass,
white part only, sliced
oil, for deep-frying

50 g mixed lettuce
leaves
1 small Lebanese
cucumber, halved
lengthways and sliced
diagonally
1 small red onion,
sliced
1/2 avocado, sliced

1. To make the salad dressing, place the garlic, peanuts, tamari, lime juice and brown sugar in a food processor or blender and process until smooth, adding 2–3 tablespoons of water to achieve the desired consistency. Transfer to a bowl.
2. Put the tofu, chives, sweet chilli sauce, kaffir lime leaves and lemon grass in a food processor and process until smooth. Transfer to a bowl and form the mixture into 12 golf

ball-sized balls.
3. Fill a wok or deep heavy-based saucepan one third full of oil and heat to 180°C (350°F), or until a cube of bread dropped into the oil browns in 15 seconds. Cook the tofu balls in batches for 2 minutes, or until browned. Remove, drain on paper towels and sprinkle with salt.
4. Put the lettuce, cucumber, onion and avocado on a serving platter and arrange the tofu balls on top. Serve immediately with the dressing.

NUTRITION PER SERVE
*Protein 15 g; Fat 30 g;
Carbohydrate 15 g; Dietary
Fibre 4.5 g; Cholesterol
0 mg; 1950 kJ (465 cal)*

Note: Shape into smaller sized balls for party fingerfood.

Tofu balls with salad

Roughly chop the tofu into large bite-sized cubes.

Process the dressing in a food processor until smooth.

With wet hands, form the tofu mixture
into even-sized balls.

Deep-fry the tofu balls in hot oil until
golden brown all over.

Pumpkin and papaya stir-fry

Preparation time:
  20 minutes
Total cooking time:
  35 minutes
Serves 4

1 tablespoon peanut oil
1 onion, sliced
2 small red chillies,
  thinly sliced
2 cloves garlic, crushed
1 star anise
1.5 kg butternut
  pumpkin, chopped
2 cups (500 ml)
  vegetable stock
450 g green papaya,
  peeled, seeded and
  grated
2 eggs, lightly beaten
1/4 cup (25 g) bean
  sprouts

1. Heat the oil in a wok over high heat, add the onion and cook for 3–5 minutes, or until translucent and golden. Add the chilli, garlic and star anise and cook for 1 minute. Add the pumpkin and cook for 1 minute.
2. Add the stock, bring to the boil, then reduce the heat to low. Simmer, partially covered, for 10–15 minutes. Cook, uncovered, for a further 10 minutes, or until the liquid has evaporated. Increase the heat to medium, add the papaya and cook for 2 minutes. Stir in the egg, remove from the heat and add the bean sprouts.

NUTRITION PER SERVE
*Protein 13 g; Fat 10 g;
Carbohydrate 42 g; Dietary
Fibre 7.5 g; Cholesterol
90 mg; 1299 kJ (310 cal)*

Phad Thai

Preparation time:
  30 minutes
Total cooking time:
  10 minutes
Serves 4

400 g dried flat
  rice-stick noodles
2 tablespoons peanut
  oil
2 eggs, lightly beaten
1 onion, thinly sliced
2 cloves garlic, crushed
1 small red capsicum,
  cut into thin strips
100 g fried tofu,
  cut into 5 mm strips
6 spring onions, thinly
  sliced on the diagonal
1/2 cup (25 g) chopped
  fresh coriander leaves
1/4 cup (60 ml) soy
  sauce
1 tablespoon soft
  brown sugar
2 teaspoons sambal
  oelek
2 tablespoons lime juice
1/4 cup (40 g) chopped
  roasted unsalted
  peanuts
1 cup (90 g) bean
  sprouts

1. Soak the noodles in a bowl of boiling water for 5–10 minutes, or until tender. Drain.
2. Heat a wok over high heat. Add enough oil to coat the side. When smoking, add the egg and swirl to form a thin omelette, then cook for 30 seconds, or until just set. Roll up, remove from the wok and slice.
3. Heat the remaining oil in the wok. Add the onion, garlic and capsicum and cook over high heat for 2–3 minutes, or until the onion softens. Add the noodles, tossing well. Stir in the tofu, omelette strips, spring onion and half the coriander.
4. Combine the soy sauce, sugar, sambal oelek and lime juice and pour in. Toss to coat the noodles. Sprinkle with the peanuts, bean sprouts and remaining coriander leaves.

NUTRITION PER SERVE
*Protein 13 g; Fat 20 g;
Carbohydrate 33 g; Dietary
Fibre 5 g; Cholesterol
90 mg; 1523 kJ (365 cal)*

*Pumpkin and papaya stir-fry (top)
and Phad Thai*

Fried caramel tempeh

Preparation time:
20 minutes
Total cooking time:
35 minutes
Serves 4

¹/3 cup (80 g) sugar
oil, for shallow-frying
250 g tempeh,
cut into 2 cm cubes
1 tablespoon oil, extra
4 red Asian shallots,
finely sliced
2 cloves garlic,
finely chopped
1 tablespoon grated
fresh ginger
1–2 small red chillies,
finely sliced
1 tablespoon soy bean
sauce
1 tablespoon lime juice
2 teaspoons grated
palm sugar

1. Place the sugar and
¹/3 cup (80 ml) water in
a small saucepan. Stir
over low heat until the
sugar has dissolved.
Bring to the boil and
cook for 5 minutes, or
until golden. Carefully
stir in ¹/2 cup (125 ml)
water and reduce the
heat to low. Cook,
stirring constantly, for
10–15 minutes, or until
thickened. Remove
from the heat.
2. Heat 1.5 cm oil in a
frying pan over high

heat. Add the tempeh
and fry in two batches,
turning occasionally,
for 5 minutes, or until
browned. Drain well.
3. Heat the extra oil
in a wok, add the
shallots, garlic, ginger
and chilli and stir-fry
over medium heat for
2 minutes, or until the
shallots are soft. Add
the tempeh, caramel
sauce and remaining
ingredients and cook
for 2 minutes.

NUTRITION PER SERVE
Protein 7.5 g; Fat 15.5 g;
Carbohydrate 22 g; Dietary
Fibre 0 g; Cholesterol
0 mg; 1100 kJ (260 cal)

Yellow pumpkin curry

Preparation time:
20 minutes
Total cooking time:
45 minutes
Serves 4

400 ml coconut cream
3–4 tablespoons Thai
yellow curry paste
2 cups (500 ml)
vegetable stock
1 kg butternut pumpkin,
cut into 3 cm cubes
2 teaspoons grated
palm sugar
1 tablespoon soy bean
sauce

2 fresh kaffir lime
leaves
2 tablespoons lime juice
540 g can bamboo
shoots, drained and
roughly chopped
440 g snake beans,
cut into 5 cm lengths
¹/2 cup (15 g) fresh
Thai basil leaves

1. Place the coconut
cream in a wok, bring
to the boil and cook
over high heat for
10–15 minutes, or until
small bubbles of oil
come to the surface—
this separating process
is called 'cracking' and
gives a thicker sauce
to the curry. Add the
curry paste and cook
for a further 5 minutes.
2. Add the stock, bring
to the boil, then add
the pumpkin, palm
sugar, soy bean sauce,
lime leaves and juice.
Reduce the heat and
simmer for 10 minutes.
Add the bamboo shoots
and beans. Cook for a
further 10–15 minutes,
or until the pumpkin
is tender and the sauce
has thickened.
3. Stir in the basil and
serve with steamed rice.

NUTRITION PER SERVE
Protein 13 g; Fat 24 g;
Carbohydrate 30 g; Dietary
Fibre 11 g; Cholesterol
1.5 mg; 1619 kJ (387 cal)

Fried caramel tempeh (top) and
Yellow pumpkin curry

Once the lemon juice and yoghurt are added to the milk it will begin to curdle.

Drain the curd mixture in a cloth-lined colander.

Saag panir

Preparation time:
  20 minutes +
  overnight refrigeration
Total cooking time:
  30 minutes
Serves 4

2 litres milk
1/3 cup (80 ml) lemon
  juice
2 tablespoons plain
  yoghurt
500 g silverbeet, cooked
2 cloves garlic
2 teaspoons grated
  fresh ginger
2 green chillies, chopped
1 onion, chopped
2 tablespoons ghee
2 teaspoons ground
  cumin
1/2 teaspoon ground
  nutmeg
3 tablespoons plain
  yoghurt, extra
1/2 cup (125 ml) cream

1. Heat the milk in a saucepan until just boiling. Reduce the heat to low, add the lemon juice and yoghurt and cook, stirring, until the mixture begins to curdle. Remove the pan from the heat and leave for 5 minutes, or until the curds start to form.
2. Line a colander with muslin or calico. Pour the curd mixture into the colander and leave until most of the liquid has drained away. Gather the muslin together and squeeze as much moisture from the curd as possible. Return to the colander, place over a bowl and refrigerate for 3 hours or overnight, until very firm and all the whey has drained away. Cut into 4 cm cubes.
3. Squeeze out any excess moisture from

the silverbeet, then finely chop.
4. Place the garlic, ginger, chilli and onion in a food processor and process until finely chopped.
5. Heat the ghee in a wok. Add the onion mixture and cook over medium heat for 5 minutes, or until the ghee begins to separate. Add the spices, extra yoghurt, 1 teaspoon salt and 1 cup (250 ml) water and simmer for 5 minutes. Transfer to the food processor, add the silverbeet and process until smooth. Return the mixture to the wok, add the curd and cream and cook for 10 minutes, or until the sauce is heated through. Serve with steamed rice.

NUTRITION PER SERVE
Protein 20 g; Fat 42 g; Carbohydrate 34 g; Dietary Fibre 1.2 g; Cholesterol 136 mg; 2457 kJ (587 cal)

Saag panir

Once the curd is firm, cut it into 4 cm bite-sized cubes.

Process the onion mixture with the silverbeet until smooth.

Balti eggplant and tofu stir-fry

Preparation time:
 15 minutes
Total cooking time:
 20 minutes
Serves 4

2 tablespoons oil
1 onion, finely chopped
¹/4 cup (70 g) balti
 curry paste
300 g slender eggplant,
 cut diagonally into
 1 cm slices
300 g firm tofu,
 cut into 1.5 cm cubes
3 ripe tomatoes,
 cut into wedges
¹/4 cup (60 ml)
 vegetable stock
75 g baby English
 spinach leaves
¹/3 cup (50 g) toasted
 cashews

1. Heat a wok or deep frying pan until very hot. Add the oil and swirl to coat. Add the onion and stir-fry over high heat for 3–4 minutes, or until softened and golden.
2. Stir in the balti paste and cook for 1 minute. Add the eggplant and cook for 5 minutes. Add the tofu, gently tossing for 3–4 minutes, or until golden.
3. Add the tomato and stock and cook for 3 minutes, or until the tomato is soft. Stir in the spinach and cook for 1–2 minutes, or until wilted. Season. Sprinkle with cashews. Serve with saffron rice.

NUTRITION PER SERVE
Protein 10 g; Fat 20 g; Carbohydrate 10 g; Dietary Fibre 4.5 g; Cholesterol 1.5 mg; 1113 kJ (265 cal)

Quick mushrooms with red curry sauce

Preparation time:
 15 minutes
Total cooking time:
 30 minutes
Serves 4

2 cups (500 ml)
 coconut cream
2 teaspoons red curry
 paste (see Note)
2 teaspoons finely
 chopped lemon grass,
 white part only
100 ml vegetable stock
1 cup (250 ml) coconut
 milk
2 teaspoons mushroom
 soy sauce
1¹/2 tablespoons shaved
 palm sugar
3 fresh kaffir lime
 leaves
1 tablespoon lime juice
400 g assorted
 mushrooms (shiitake,
 oyster, enoki, button)
2 tablespoons fresh
 coriander leaves
3 tablespoons torn
 fresh Thai basil

1. Place the coconut cream in a wok, bring to the boil and cook over high heat for 10–15 minutes, or until small bubbles of oil come to the surface— this separating process is called 'cracking'. Add the curry paste and lemon grass and cook, stirring continuously, for 3–4 minutes, or until fragrant.
2. Reduce the heat to medium, add the stock, coconut milk, soy sauce, palm sugar, kaffir lime leaves and lime juice. Cook, stirring, for 3–4 minutes, or until the sugar has dissolved. Stir in the mushrooms and cook for 3–4 minutes, or until tender.
3. Remove from the heat and stir in the coriander and basil. Serve with steamed rice.

NUTRITION PER SERVE
Protein 7.5 g; Fat 40 g; Carbohydrate 17 g; Dietary Fibre 6 g; Cholesterol 1 mg; 1877 kJ (450 cal)

Note: Ensure the curry paste doesn't contain shrimp paste.

Balti eggplant and tofu stir-fry (top) and Quick mushrooms with red curry sauce

Thai green papaya salad

Preparation time:
40 minutes
Total cooking time:
Nil
Serves 4

500 g green papaya,
   peeled and seeded
1–2 small red chillies,
   thinly sliced
1 tablespoon grated
   palm sugar
1 tablespoon soy bean
   sauce
2 tablespoons lime
   juice
1 tablespoon fried
   garlic (see Note)
1 tablespoon fried
   shallots (see Note)
50 g green beans,
   cut into 1 cm lengths
8 cherry tomatoes,
   quartered
2 tablespoons chopped
   roasted unsalted
   peanuts

1. Grate the papaya
into long, fine shreds
with a zester or a knife.
2. Place the papaya in a
large mortar and pestle
or food processor with
the chilli, palm sugar,
soy bean sauce and
lime juice. Lightly
pound until combined.
Add the fried garlic

and shallots, beans and
tomatoes. Lightly pound
for a further minute, or
until combined. Serve
immediately, sprinkled
with the peanuts.

NUTRITION PER SERVE
*Protein 4.5 g; Fat 5.5 g;
Carbohydrate 24 g; Dietary
Fibre 4.5 g; Cholesterol
0 mg; 680 kJ (160 cal)*

Note: Packets of fried
garlic and shallots are
available from Asian
food stores.

Grilled eggplant with miso

Preparation time:
20 minutes +
30 minutes standing
Total cooking time:
20 minutes
Serves 4

3 eggplants, cut into
   2 cm round slices
oil, for brushing
1/4 cup (75 g) white
   miso
2 tablespoons mirin
2 tablespoons light soy
   sauce
2 tablespoons sugar
sesame seeds and grated
   daikon, to garnish

Dressing
1/4 cup (60 ml) light
   soy sauce

1 tablespoon rice
   vinegar or white
   vinegar
1 teaspoon sesame oil
1 tablespoon mirin
1 teaspoon sugar

1. Sprinkle the eggplant
slices with salt and
leave in a colander for
30 minutes. Rinse
under running water
and pat dry with paper
towels. Brush the
eggplant slices with
oil and cook under a
hot grill for 7 minutes
on each side, or until
golden and the eggplant
is tender.
2. Place the miso, mirin,
soy sauce and sugar in
a small bowl and mix
together.
3. Reduce the grill to
low. Brush one side of
the eggplant with the
miso mixture and grill
for 1–2 minutes, or
until the mixture is just
dry, being careful not to
burn the mixture.
4. To make the dressing,
combine the soy sauce,
vinegar, sesame oil,
mirin and sugar in a
small bowl. Place the
eggplant in a serving
dish, pour on the
dressing and garnish
with the sesame seeds
and grated daikon.

NUTRITION PER SERVE
*Protein 3.5 g; Fat 7.5 g;
Carbohydrate 16 g; Dietary
Fibre 3.5 g; Cholesterol
0 mg; 610 kJ (145 cal)*

*Thai green papaya salad (top)
and Grilled eggplant with miso*

Spicy Indonesian tempeh

Preparation time:
  20 minutes
Total cooking time:
  25 minutes
Serves 4

oil, for shallow-frying
250 g tempeh, sliced
1 tablespoon oil, extra
4 red Asian shallots,
  finely sliced
2–3 birds-eye chillies,
  finely chopped
2 cloves garlic, finely
  sliced
2 teaspoons grated
  fresh galangal
1 stem lemon grass,
  white part only, sliced
2 fresh kaffir lime leaves
2 tablespoons shaved
  palm sugar
1 tablespoon kecap
  manis

1. Heat 1.5 cm oil in a large frying pan over high heat. Cook the tempeh in batches for 1–2 minutes, or until lightly browned. Drain.
2. Heat the extra oil in a wok, add the shallots, chilli and garlic. Cook over medium heat for 3 minutes, or until soft. Add the remaining ingredients and 1/3 cup (80 ml) water and cook for 2 minutes.
3. Reduce the heat, add the tempeh and simmer

for 5–10 minutes, or until heated through. Add a little water, if necessary, to prevent any sticking.

NUTRITION PER SERVE
Protein 5 g; Fat 15 g; Carbohydrate 0 g; Dietary Fibre 0 g; Cholesterol 0 mg; 750 kJ (180 cal)

Vegetable dumplings

Preparation time:
  30 minutes
Total cooking time:
  15 minutes
Makes 25

1 tablespoon oil
3 spring onions, sliced
2 cloves garlic, chopped
2 teaspoons grated
  fresh ginger
3 tablespoons chopped
  fresh garlic chives
420 g choy sum,
  shredded
2 tablespoons sweet
  chilli sauce
3 tablespoons chopped
  fresh coriander leaves
1/4 cup (45 g) water
  chestnuts, drained and
  chopped
25 gow gee wrappers

Dipping sauce
1/2 teaspoon sesame oil
1/2 teaspoon peanut oil
1 tablespoon soy sauce

1 tablespoon lime juice
1 small red chilli, finely
  chopped

1. Heat the oil in a frying pan and cook the spring onion, garlic, ginger and chives over medium heat for 1–2 minutes, or until soft. Add the choy sum and cook over high heat for 4–5 minutes, or until wilted. Stir in the chilli sauce, coriander and water chestnuts. Cool. If the mixture is too wet, squeeze dry.
2. Lay a wrapper on the work surface. Place a heaped teaspoon of the filling in the centre. Moisten the edge of the pastry with water and pinch to seal, forming a ball. Trim. Repeat with the remaining wrappers and filling.
3. Half fill a wok with water and bring to the boil. Line a bamboo steamer with baking paper. Steam the dumplings, seam-side down, for 5–6 minutes.
4. To make the dipping sauce, combine all the ingredients. Serve with the dumplings.

NUTRITION PER DUMPLING
Protein 2 g; Fat 1 g; Carbohydrate 2 g; Dietary Fibre 1 g; Cholesterol 0 mg; 84 kJ (20 cal)

Spicy Indonesian tempeh (top) and Vegetable dumplings

Mix together all the prepared vegetables in a bowl.

Loosely stir the batter with chopsticks—
it should still be lumpy.

Vegetable tempura patties

Preparation time:
25 minutes
Total cooking time:
15 minutes
Serves 4

Wasabi mayonnaise
2 teaspoons wasabi
paste
1 teaspoon Japanese
soy sauce
1/2 cup (125 g) whole-
egg mayonnaise
1 teaspoon sake

1/2 carrot, julienned
1/2 onion, finely sliced
100 g orange sweet
potato, grated
1 small zucchini, grated
1 small potato,
julienned
4 spring onions,
green part included,
cut into 2 cm lengths

4 nori sheets, shredded
2 cups (250 g) tempura
flour, sifted
2 cups (250 ml) chilled
soda water
oil, for deep-frying
2 tablespoons shredded
pickled ginger

1. To make the wasabi mayonnaise, place the wasabi paste, soy sauce, mayonnaise and sake in a small bowl and stir together well. Set aside.
2. To make the patties, place the carrot, onion, orange sweet potato, zucchini, potato, spring onion and nori in a bowl. Toss together.
3. Place the tempura flour into a large bowl and make a well in the centre. Add the soda water and loosely mix together with chopsticks or a fork until just combined—the batter should still be lumpy.

Add the vegetables and quickly fold through until just combined.
4. Fill a wok or deep heavy-based saucepan one third full of oil and heat to 180°C (350°F), or until a cube of bread dropped into the oil browns in 15 seconds.
5. Gently drop 1/4 cup (60 ml) of the vegetable mixture into the oil, making sure that the patty is not too compact, and cook for 1–2 minutes, or until golden and crisp. Drain on paper towels and season with sea salt. Repeat with the remaining mixture to make 12 patties. Serve immediately, topped with the wasabi mayonnaise and the pickled ginger.

NUTRITION PER SERVE
Protein 5.8 g; Fat 20 g;
Carbohydrate 64 g; Dietary
Fibre 3.5 g; Cholesterol
10 mg; 1948 kJ (465 cal)

Vegetable tempura patties

Gently drop the vegetable patty mixture into the hot oil.

Deep-fry the patties until lightly brown and crisp.

Asian barley pilau

Preparation time:
  10 minutes +
  15 minutes soaking
Total cooking time:
  35 minutes
Serves 4

*15 g dried sliced
  Chinese mushrooms
2 cups (500 ml) stock
1/2 cup (125 ml) sherry
1 tablespoon oil
3 large red Asian
  shallots, sliced
2 cloves garlic, crushed
1 teaspoon Sichuan
  peppercorns, crushed
1 tablespoon grated
  fresh ginger
1 1/2 cups (330 g) pearl
  barley
500 g choy sum,
  cut into 5 cm lengths
3 teaspoons kecap manis
1 teaspoon sesame oil*

1. Soak the mushrooms
in boiling water for
15 minutes. Drain and
reserve 1/2 cup (125 ml)
of the liquid.
2. Place the stock and
sherry in a saucepan
and keep at a simmer.
3. Heat the oil in a
saucepan and cook the
shallots over medium
heat for 2–3 minutes,
or until soft. Add the
garlic, peppercorns
and ginger and cook
for 1 minute. Stir in the
barley and mushrooms.

Stir in the stock mixture
and mushroom liquid.
Reduce the heat and
simmer, covered, for
25 minutes, or until the
liquid evaporates.
4. Steam the choy sum
until wilted. Stir in the
barley mixture, kecap
manis and sesame oil.

NUTRITION PER SERVE
*Protein 14 g; Fat 8.5 g;
Carbohydrate 52 g; Dietary
Fibre 14 g; Cholesterol
0 mg; 1567 kJ (375 cal)*

Vegetable donburi

Preparation time:
  20 minutes +
  15 minutes soaking
Total cooking time:
  35 minutes
Serves 4

*2 cups (440 g) short-
  grain white rice
10 g dried whole
  shiitake mushrooms
2 tablespoons oil
1 onion, sliced
2 slender eggplants,
  sliced on the diagonal
100 g green beans,
  cut into 4 cm lengths
5 spring onions,
  cut into 2 cm lengths
100 ml Japanese soy
  sauce
100 ml mirin
1/4 cup (60 g) sugar
4 eggs, lightly beaten*

1. Wash the rice and
place in a saucepan
with 2 1/2 cups (625 ml)
water. Bring to the boil,
reduce the heat and
simmer, covered, for
15 minutes. Leave,
covered, for 10 minutes.
2. Soak the mushrooms
in 1 2/3 cups (410 ml)
boiling water for
15 minutes. Drain and
reserve the liquid.
Remove the stems and
cut the caps in half.
3. Heat the oil in a
deep frying pan. Cook
the onion over medium
heat for 4 minutes. Add
the eggplant and cook
for 3–4 minutes, or
until softened. Add the
beans, mushrooms and
spring onion and cook
for 2–3 minutes, or
until almost cooked.
Combine the soy sauce,
mushroom liquid, mirin
and sugar, and stir
through the vegetables.
Simmer for 4 minutes.
4. Pour the egg over the
vegetables, cover and
simmer for 1 minute,
or until partly cooked.
Serve the rice in bowls,
spoon on the vegetable
mixture and pour on
the cooking sauce.

NUTRITION PER SERVE
*Protein 10 g; Fat 15 g;
Carbohydrate 15 g; Dietary
Fibre 4 g; Cholesterol
180 mg; 976 kJ (233 cal)*

*Asian barley pilau (top)
and Vegetable donburi*

Wrap a strip of nori around each
mushroom and dampen to seal.

Deep-fry the orange sweet potato ribbons
in hot oil until golden all over.

Seaweed-wrapped fried mushrooms

Preparation time:
  30 minutes
Total cooking time:
  15 minutes
Serves 4

Sauce
1/3 cup (80 ml)
  purchased sushi
  dipping sauce
100 ml mirin
2 teaspoons grated
  fresh ginger
2 teaspoons sugar

3 nori sheets
12 cap mushrooms,
  stalks removed
400 g orange sweet
  potato
oil, for deep-frying
225 ml chilled soda
  water
1 egg, lightly
  beaten

1 cup (125 g) tempura
  flour
2 tablespoons wasabi
  powder

1. To make the sauce, place the sushi dipping sauce, mirin, ginger, sugar and 1 tablespoon water in a saucepan and stir over medium heat until the sugar has dissolved. Cover and keep warm.
2. Cut the nori sheets into twelve 4 cm wide strips with scissors. Wrap a strip around each mushroom, dampening the end to help it stick. Cut the orange sweet potato into ribbon strips with a vegetable peeler.
3. Fill a deep heavy-based frying pan one third full of oil and heat to 190°C (375°F), or until a cube of bread dropped into the oil

browns in 10 seconds. Cook the sweet potato in batches for about 30–60 seconds, or until golden and crispy. Drain on paper towels, season and keep warm.
4. Place the soda water and egg in a large bowl and whisk well. Add the tempura flour and wasabi powder and loosely mix in with chopsticks or a fork until just combined— the batter should still be lumpy. Coat the mushrooms in the batter and cook in batches for 1–2 minutes, or until golden and crisp, turning once. Drain on paper towels and season with salt. Serve immediately with the sweet potato ribbons and the sauce.

NUTRITION PER SERVE
Protein 6.5 g; Fat 12 g; Carbohydrate 48 g; Dietary Fibre 3.5 g; Cholesterol 45 mg; 1357 kJ (324 cal)

Seaweed-wrapped fried mushrooms

Dip each seaweed-wrapped mushroom in the tempura batter using chopsticks.

Deep-fry the mushrooms in hot oil until golden and crisp.

Indian chickpea stew

Preparation time:
  20 minutes +
  overnight soaking
Total cooking time:
  1 hour 50 minutes
Serves 6

1¹/2 cups (330 g)
  chickpeas
2 teaspoons garam
  masala
2 teaspoons ground
  cumin
2 teaspoons ground
  coriander
20 g ghee or butter
1 onion, chopped
2 cloves garlic, crushed
1 teaspoon ground
  turmeric
1 tablespoon grated
  fresh ginger
810 g can chopped
  tomatoes
³/4 cup (185 ml)
  vegetable stock
2 cups (80 g) chopped
  English spinach
2 tablespoons chopped
  fresh coriander leaves

1. Soak the chickpeas
in cold water overnight,
then drain. Place in a
large saucepan, cover
with water and bring
to the boil. Cook for
1–1¹/2 hours, or until
tender. Drain.
2. Dry-fry the garam
masala, ground cumin
and coriander in a
frying pan over medium
heat for 1 minute.
3. Heat the ghee in a
large saucepan. Add the
fried spices, onion,
garlic, turmeric and
ginger and cook over
medium heat, stirring,
for 5–6 minutes, or
until the onion is soft.
Add the chickpeas and
tomato. Reduce the
heat and simmer for
10 minutes. Place 2 cups
(500 ml) of the mixture
and the stock in a food
processor and process
until smooth. Return to
the pan, add the spinach
and coriander and cook
until wilted. Season.

NUTRITION PER SERVE
*Protein 11 g; Fat 6.5 g;
Carbohydrate 25 g; Dietary
Fibre 9.5 g; Cholesterol
8.5 mg; 864 kJ (205 cal)*

Asian greens with coconut rice

Preparation time:
  10 minutes +
  10 minutes standing
Total cooking time:
  30 minutes
Serves 4

1 tablespoon oil
2 stems lemon grass,
  white part only,
  bruised and cut into
  5 cm lengths
1 clove garlic, crushed
2 teaspoons grated
  fresh ginger
1 cup (200 g) jasmine
  rice
1 cup (250 ml) coconut
  milk
2–3 fresh kaffir lime
  leaves, crushed
800 g Chinese broccoli,
  halved lengthways
2 tablespoons kecap
  manis
1 tablespoon lime juice

1. Heat the oil in a
saucepan over medium
heat. Add the lemon
grass, garlic and ginger
and cook for 2 minutes
(do not burn). Stir in
the rice for 2 minutes,
or until coated.
2. Add the coconut
milk, lime leaves and
2 cups (500 ml) water.
Cook, covered, over low
heat for 15–20 minutes,
or until the rice is
tender and the liquid is
absorbed. Cover and
leave for 10 minutes.
3. Steam the broccoli
until just wilted. Place
on a platter and drizzle
with the combined
kecap manis and lime
juice. Serve with the
coconut rice.

NUTRITION PER SERVE
*Protein 14 g; Fat 16 g;
Carbohydrate 42 g; Dietary
Fibre 10 g; Cholesterol
0 mg; 1544 kJ (370 cal)*

---

*Indian chickpea stew (top) and
Asian greens with coconut rice*

Index